LIFE AND JOURNEYINGS IN CENTRAL AUSTRALIA

By
J. C. FINLAYSON

ETT IMPRINT
Exile Bay

ETT IMPRINT
PO Box R1906
Royal Exchange NSW 1225 Australia

ISBN 978-1-923024-10-6 (paper)
ISBN 978-1-923024-11-3 (ebook

Cover image: Afghans and Camels at Oonadatta 1919

Cover and internal images designed by Tom Thompson

FOREWORD

MUCH is being said at the present time for and against the construction of an overland railway, the possibility of large tracts of so-called desert country carrying stock and providing a supply of water from underground, and climatic conditions for the settlement of white people in the interior.

This little book merely deals with what was my own experience during a sojourn of two and a half years in the centre of Australia.

J. C. F.

J. C. FINLAYSON.

Chapter I

A PEEP AT OODNADATTA

SIX hundred and eighty-eight miles north of Adelaide, in the State of South Australia, and at the terminus of the Great Northern Railway, is the village of Oodnadatta.

At the time of which I write, 1914-1916, it is a quiet, well-conducted little village—police station, railway station and residence, public school, doctor's residence, hotel, butcher, baker, three general stores, a boarding house. These, with twenty-three private houses, including the home of the nursing sister, known as The Hostel, make up this little village of white people.

The men live and work and rest and look out for the latest news, as do men in all places.

The women do their home duties, with the help of native women, visit each other in the afternoons, and attend to the needs of their husbands and children in the evening.

Stockmen and drovers sit about on the boarding-house and hotel verandahs, and in their quiet, thoughtful way tell bush stories and discuss the weather. Others are quite done up with weeks of travel with stock, working in the saddle day and night. These go off quietly to rest. Others again

STOCK YARD.

are letter writing. for as they go to their distant stations it may be months before they are in touch with a mail again.

The children attend their school. and when a clergyman pays a visit to the village the people attend Sabbath service in the schoolroom.

Almost every home has a piano. and everybody plays and sings. Altogether it is about the most intelligent. well-conducted little village it were possible to find.

Water is laid on all over the village from an artesian bore. and some few have tanks for rain water. The bore water is mineral. and is at times almost boiling.

Once a fortnight the passenger train comes North. arriving at Oodnadatta on Friday night. and departing again for the South on Tuesday morning. For about eight months of the year this is supplemented by stock trains. which carry mails. and upon which one may travel on urgent business by special permit.

Supplies are easily brought from Adelaide.

Although the medical man has the right of a private practice. the railway employees from Oodnadatta to Hergott Springs. inclusive. have the first claim upon his time.

In addition to the white population. there are also a number of natives. the women being employed as domestic helps and the men and boys as messengers. wood-cutters and yardmen. All of these. although employed in the village during the day. go to their

Annie leaving camp to go walk-about.

Aboriginal camp at Oodnadatta.

own camp, about a mile distant, at sundown, and after the night's rest return at sunrise to their various duties.

Also, there is a settlement of Afghans about half-a-mile distant in another direction, of which one hears very little except that it is a busy centre for the loading and unloading of camels. The Afghan is the expert camel man, and he has his own camels. So that when the train from the South brings up goods and provisions to Oodnadatta for them, they take them to their own settlement, and with experienced hands do their loading. Also they are employed by the storekeepers to carry their goods: these they load at the different stores.

These strings of camels set out in all directions to the interior beyond the railway for hundreds of miles carrying flour, tea, sugar and all that is needed by those brave white settlers. The Afghan is a generous, thrifty, sober person.

CHAPTER II

JOURNEYING NORTH

IN February of the year 1914 I left my home city
of Melbourne for that distant outpost, knowing
nothing of the country to which I was going,
knowing nothing of the people, knowing nothing
of the conditions. But as I said farewell to friends
at Spencer Street station, when the Adelaide express
steamed out. hope was high in me—hope sometimes is.

After an all-night journey of five hundred and
sixty miles to Adelaide, the first stage was passed.
At Adelaide I met with friends and stayed for the
night, the next day boarding the Great Northern
train for the further journey of six hundred and
eighty-eight miles to the Interior.

South Australia is a beautiful country, and I have
not seen anything in any of the other States to
come up to their railways and refreshment rooms as
far as Quorn.

Arrived at Quorn, we went to the hotel, where
all guests were received by a kindly, genial host and
his happy, smiling wife, who took me to my room.
I was very hot, very dusty, and very tired after that
long journey, and to arrive at a well-managed, well-

NATIVES

conducted, comfortable hotel was a great pleasure. Everything was cool and clean and fresh.

After dressing for dinner we entered a large dining room, and were supplied with one of the best dinners one could wish for, our host and his wife personally superintending to see that their guests received of their best.

Although Quorn is coast country, there was an air, or a new kind of atmosphere, which I had not previously known. During the meal I listened to cheerful chatter, and witnessed the happy, free way in which old friends met. One going North and another South, one going East and another West. But whatever point of the compass they come from, or are going to, they are all happy and friendly. Nobody waits for an introduction before speaking in this friendly country. A stranger is recognised at once, and is given a friendly nod and " Good day." Others will extend a hand and ask if one is not a stranger in these parts, and offer useful information.

Before retiring we spent the evening on the hotel balcony, listening to a band and viewing the beautiful hills which are on the North and West of Quorn.

Having spent a quiet and restful night, we set out on the North-going train on our second day's journey, the early part of which takes us through the graceful curves which wind in and out skirting the Flinders Range. This is very picturesque and pleasant.

Later, as one goes on from one small settlement to another, one comes out into open, sandy country. The stopping places vary in size and importance. At some few there is quite a fine village and station building. At others just a siding with a few scattered houses. At others, again, there is no house to be seen, and a step-ladder is placed beside the train to allow some family to alight and carry off their luggage.

But at one and all the interest in the fortnightly train is just the same. Hotelkeepers, storekeepers, station men, drovers, women and children, Afghans in black, white and red turbans, groups of natives in varied costumes, appear. All are alike curious to see who is on the train. We peep out to see this new country and its people.

The day is growing very hot as we grind on weary mile after weary mile, with limbs and back aching, and nothing but hard wooden seats to give rest. We welcome lunch time, when there is a stop.

There is no refreshment room, but a kindly stationmaster's wife spares us some boiling water for our tea. It is a short rest, and on we go again to grind through more sand and to battle with dust and heat and flies.

Through it all we are happy and interested. Everybody looks happy, and each fresh person we meet gives us a friendly bush greeting and welcoming smile. Little dusky children peep from behind the hiding place of their mother's skirts. I smile and try to get them out into the open, but it is no use, they are timid, shy creatures. They recognise a penny, however, and know that it will buy sweets, for which they have a fancy. Seeing their dark eyes fixed on the penny, I toss a few on the ground, when immediately little black and brown naked forms dart out and pounce upon them, then rush back to their laughing mothers. Those who get the pennies do not keep them to themselves, but share with the others.

As we bump onward we are very hot and very thirsty, sand in our eyes and grating between our teeth, so that we need frequently to make tea, which is the favourite and apparently the best drink.

A fellow-traveller—himself parched with the heat—appears at our open carriage door and asks, " Would you like tea? " We would indeed. So we put tea in our pots and hand them to him, and almost before the train draws up he has jumped to the ground and is seen speeding along to the engine for boiling water. Back he comes again, and hurriedly giving us our tea, he races off again to the little wayside hotel for a drink of cool ale, or some tea, or perhaps he will stay and share our tea and hamper.

The train does not need to wait for us to finish our meal, for we have with us all that we need of our own things, and we take our time, so in a few minutes we have passed on again.

As the day advances into late afternoon, a strong wind is rising, and by the time we are approaching Hergott Springs we are overtaken by the beginning of a dust-storm.

THE TELEGRAPH STATION.

Onward the driver races his train in an endeavour to beat the gale. He knows this country, and knows that if the worst of the storm overtakes us before we get to Hergott Springs he cannot take his train through it.

We arrive, and our valiant driver has won. Ready hands are there to help as we tumble out on to the little platform, and quickly grasp such luggage as we may need for the one night. Then we put down our heads and run for the hotel, dodging as we go flying tins and sticks and scampering goats.

Our kind host is all concern for us as he shuts up doors and windows in a futile effort to keep out the flying sand. However, the storm is here, and there is nothing to do but to put up with it, so we get off some of our hot clothes and get into something light and cool, then go down stairs to a good dinner—yes, it is a good dinner, in spite of its bits of sand.

We are told that we are " in for a bad night," and we hurry through with our meal and return to our rooms. There is dust everywhere; my hair is full of it, my clothes are full of it, and the doors and windows are powerless to keep out the flying sand.

It is only nine o'clock, but I settle into bed and cover up my head and try to breathe with some degree of comfort and get a little rest. All night long the storm blows and rages, and rattles, carrying everything before it, till towards dawn it calmed down, and we got a little rest.

After such a night it was surprising to find the new day dawn bright and calm and clear.

After breakfast and many apologies from our host on account of the weather. we stepped out briskly for the railway station. where our train engine had already got up steam and was puffing loudly in impatience to be off on the last stage of that journey.

It is no easy task, the taking of a train over a line just swept by a dust-storm, so we were told that there was need of haste, and with waving of hands, exchanging of parcels and giving and taking of messages, we drew. out from Hergott Springs.

It was not long before I found out why we had needed to make an early start. Sections of the line ahead of us were completely covered up by drifting sand. Gangs of men were already out working hard with shovels to clear a way for the train to pass. And on and still further on gangs were at work. Sometimes they had it clear before the train came on, at others our train had just to wait till a way was cleared—and we had several such waits, which we occupied in an endeavour to keep reasonably cool.

The country all along this stage is flat, and appears barren till one comes upon a spring surrounded by date palms—just one solitary oasis. Here and there grow clusters of that beautiful bright red and black bloom, the Sturt Pea. All else looks flat, with sand ridges covered with salt bush and shrubs.

At each little wayside place the loading and unloading of camels and donkey teams is going on. And as we grind along on wheels we pass strings of camels making their way to the North, their Afghan masters in the lead and native boy behind.

Sister Jean Williamson, Oonadatta, 1916.

As we pass by isolated cottages clusters of a few white or black children stand about. Or perhaps one gets a glimpse of some lonely white woman at her work. If we have any books or papers, we throw them out in passing, in the hope of bringing her a little cheer.

On the whole journey from Hergott Springs to Oodnadatta there is no place where one might purchase a meal, so we go through the same process of tea-making with water from the engine, as on the previous day, and the hamper meal.

There is such a thirsty company that our cups are soon used up, and men approach the teapot with empty tins, billy lids—anything so that they might ease that thirst. Quench it? No! This is the last meal before we reach our destination, so we carefully pack away all our cups, knives, etc., into a basket, and once more settle down to being ground and bumped along to the end of the journey, which we reached late at night, after having been fifteen hours in the train.

On arriving at Oodnadatta the train was met by the whole village. I put out my head from a window and peer along the half-dark station platform. Is there anybody to meet me? But already the young agent had jumped on to the train and was offering me a welcome and gathering up my luggage.

On the platform I am met by the nursing sister whom I have come to relieve at the hospital.

We are soon on our way walking over to the boarding house where, in spite of the lateness of the hour, a good dinner is provided.

All around seemed fragrant with bush kindliness; drovers from the North met stockmen from the South, parents met their children, and women rejoined their husbands, each one bringing news from distant friends, or having some new experience to relate.

It was a happy gathering, but it was with a feeling of relief that I stepped over the street to the Hostel, which was to be my home for eighteen months.

"Y" 151 arrives at Oonadatta in 1917.

CHAPTER III

PATIENTS

AFTER a night of perfect rest I awakened late, to find that the village had been astir for several hours. The Sister came in with my letters and breakfast, and showed anxiety to hand over the responsibility of things to me, so that she might have time to pack and bid farewell to her many friends before starting on her journey South in three days' time.

Looking out of my window, I see already the camel mail setting out for the silent North, whence it journeys three hundred and fifty miles beyond the railway, delivering its mails for East and West as it goes steadily North.

For three days Oodnadatta is a very busy place; the train has come in on Friday night and will be leaving for the South again early on Tuesday morning.

In a very short time I have made myself acquainted with the few people of the village and written to friends at home and in Adelaide.

The Hostel is a corrugated iron bungalow of six rooms, dispensary and one large ward, surrounded on its four sides by a wide verandah. It stands on a good block of land, and has a lawn of grass kept green all the year by a plentiful supply of bore water and a hose.

As Sister-in-charge I lived quite alone, and was free to have daily use of a native woman as help. It was my business to attend any sick in the village and to have entire care of any in the Hostel. If a case required a doctor I called him in. But it often happened that on such occasions the doctor would be many miles away on railway business; indeed, some of the worst accidents happened when I could not get the doctor for some days.

During the intense heat of February, as I sat one day beneath the shelter of my verandah writing letters and doing battle with flies, a native boy opened the gate and handed me a telegram. On opening it I found that it had been sent from a telegraph station three hundred and fifty miles to the North. " Please send lotion for sore eyes, infected from flies. Urgent." I looked at my watch; yes, I had missed the North mail by just two hours, and there would not be another for two weeks, and then it would take eleven days more to get there—in all, twenty-five days.

Going at once to the telegraph station, I wired to the man that his message had come too late, and gave instructions regarding treatment of the eye— there being no doctor in the village at that time.

Returning to the dispensary, I made up a parcel of the necessary lotion and dressings, and kept them ready to hand to the first man that I could find going North who might overtake the mail.

Bill and Harry Gepp with their Aboriginal Nurse, Bobalinda;
and the family dog, Oonadatta 1917.

On receiving my reply, the man had decided to at once set out on the journey South as fast as horses could bring him over all those miles of dry country, troubled all the way by the intense heat, flies and dust. This took him eleven days to accomplish, and when he at last arrived it was found that the eye had burst, and there was little to do beyond sending him on the further six hundred and eighty-eight miles to Adelaide, for operation, by the first cattle train going South.

Another case I recall which impressed me with the need for medical help further North was that of a little child who had met with an accident. The little sufferer came to us over hundreds of miles. This also we were unable to deal with, not having an X-ray, and owing to the lapse of time since the accident.

We took it into the hospital, however, and did all that we could to relieve it. A few days later I went with the child to Hergott Springs, where I sat with it in my arms all night, and the next day placed it in the South-going train in the care of its parents, I myself returning to Oodnadatta on a cattle train.

Again I recall the case of another little child, just a mite a few days old; with but slight warning its newly-given life passed out. And being an only son, its life had been very precious.

The sick and troubled mother asked me to bury her babe. Now, it had never occurred to me that I might ever be called upon to perform such a service.

The smith and carpenter prepared a tiny white casket, in which we placed the sleeping babe. The old grandmother plucked from her little cottage garden such flowers that she had.

Covered by a rug, the little casket was conveyed in a spring cart. I, accompanied by two other women, followed in a buggy to some little distance from the village to the burial ground, marked only by broken fences and a few mounds of earth.

At the graveside we were met by a young man, hat in hand, leaning upon a shovel.

Using the reins from the horse, this man, with the help of the driver, lowered the little casket into its resting place.

Out in that desert place, with the wind howling through the oaks, we five, half-blinded by the flying sand, stood around while I read from " The Bushman's Companion " the service.

What days, weeks and months of anxiety do men and women of the Inland endure wondering will all be well for the mother and her helpless babe.

Even here at the gateway one wonders at the splendid courage with which they face danger to themselves and their children—what of those who have penetrated hundreds of miles beyond the head of the railway?

The tooth extractions of most of the white people I found long overdue, and their health suffering in consequence. The natives have strong teeth, difficult to extract. Those of the Afghan, on the other hand, being very simple to extract. That was my experience, but it may not be general. I did nearly one hundred extractions in two years.

old grandmother plucked from her little cottage garden such flowers that she had.

Covered by a rug, the little casket was conveyed in a spring cart. I, accompanied by two other women, followed in a buggy to some little distance from the village to the burial ground, marked only by broken fences and a few mounds of earth.

At the graveside we were met by a young man, hat in hand, leaning upon a shovel.

Using the reins from the horse, this man, with the help of the driver, lowered the little casket into its resting place.

Out in that desert place, with the wind howling through the oaks, we five, half-blinded by the flying sand, stood around while I read from " The Bushman's Companion " the service.

What days, weeks and months of anxiety do men and women of the Inland endure wondering will all be well for the mother and her helpless babe.

Even here at the gateway one wonders at the splendid courage with which they face danger to themselves and their children—what of those who have penetrated hundreds of miles beyond the head of the railway?

The tooth extractions of most of the white people I found long overdue, and their health suffering in consequence. The natives have strong teeth, difficult to extract. Those of the Afghan, on the other hand, being very simple to extract. That was my experience, but it may not be general. I did nearly one hundred extractions in two years.

The possibility of a nursing sister living at Alice Springs had long been spoken of, and a definite request came to me from the superintendent: "Would I go to Alice Springs and just live there for one year, then report as to conditions and advisableness of building a nursing home in this little settlement in the heart of the Macdonnell Ranges?"

After much correspondence it was decided that I should go. And in due time arrangements were made for my stay there—very inadequate arrangements, but the best that could be done. I would go in the interests of the sick. Those in the North urged me to go, while many others about me urged me—in my own interest—not to go. However, there was only one way of finding out what we wished to know, and I held to my original decision to make the attempt.

Mother and baby at home, Oonadatta, 1917.

CHAPTER IV

FARTHER NORTH

THE opportunity for travelling came at last. A lady from Adelaide would be going North in a couple of weeks to join her husband, and would I like to travel with her? I would be glad to do so, for urgent calls were coming from sick people in the North, and I was assured of a warm welcome. So I hurried on with arrangements for handing over the Hostel as it had been handed over to me eighteen months before. At length the day for departure arrived.

The lady with whom I was to travel had come up from Adelaide, bringing on the train with her a new buggy and new harness. A stockman who had come down to truck cattle at the railway had delivered his stock and was now ready for his return journey into the Interior again, and had undertaken to drive us.

When a bushman undertakes to convey ladies on a journey of this kind, he does things properly, so we could safely leave all arrangements in his hands.

After much excitement of packing clothes and food and saying of farewells, the hour arrived for us to start.

As we two city women stood at the Hostel gate, up drove the cavalcade of pack horses, attended by a native boy, and headed by the buggy with its four horses, two in the pole and two in the lead.

My companion climbed up to the seat beside the driver, while I clambered up behind and perched side-

TROUGHS FOR WATERING STOCK.

ways, high on top of the luggage and bedding. There I sat feeling like a barrel organ monkey.

Half the village was out to see us start off, and amidst shouts of farewell and warnings that I should be " back in three weeks," we plunged forward, rattling over the stones, and in a short time were leaving the village behind us, while our lively horses carried us forward into the—to us—unknown.

On and on we raced, till after travelling twenty miles we drew up, made a fire, and had a hurried lunch, put fresh horses in, and on we went again for another long stretch till we drew up beside a solitary tree for the night camp, having left Oodnadatta forty miles behind us.

Our driver was one of the best, and throughout the whole of that long journey to the centre he did all in his power for our comfort.

The native boys, after attending to the horses with food, drink and hobbles, at once set about putting up our tent.

The night was very cold, and after a meal we talked by the fire for a little time, then filling our rubber hot water bags from the kettle on the camp fire, we retired to our tent and were soon tucked up into our camp beds. But we were not warm; the cold air seemed to go through everything.

The native boys were camped some distance away, and our driver, rolled up in blankets and rug beside the camp fire, between our tent and the natives.

We were too cold to sleep—it was the month of August—so we tried to cheer each other with jokes and stories of home. As the night wore on wild dogs could be heard in the distance, howling. We sprang up alarmed, and had some idea of calling to the driver; but peaceful snores from a bundle rolled up somewhere about the dying camp fire gave us no encouragement to do this, so we crept back to our cold bunks.

The next alarm was caused by a camel with a dull bell on plunging around our tent in hobbles. This creature had come from a neighbouring camp to explore, and was part of an Afghan's outfit.

We were afraid—afraid of the great silence—but tried hard to get to sleep, till some slight sound brought us with one flying leap to the tent door together, each one asking " What was it? " Nothing to be seen except space, and nothing to hear but a great silence. We each silently had visions of armed warriors making a night attack, but crept back again and lay and listened alert for any emergency.

Through weary nights of watching the sick I have often longed for the dawn; but never before, nor since, have I welcomed that pale streak in the East as I did after that first night in a bush camp.

Early as we came forth from our tent, our driver had already got a fire and prepared breakfast, the native boys being out after the horses.

There was need for haste, as the time for heavy rains was at hand, and if it came before we passed over the many dry creek beds they would be roaring streams of water, and, for the present, our further progress impossible.

So that our anxious guide urged us to greater haste—he had a great responsibility to deliver us safely.

We were quickly ready, and our tent was taken down by the native boys and rolled up to continue

"AFTER THAT FIRST NIGHT IN A BUSH CAMP."

the journey. Our breakfast of boiled eggs was soon over, and all was ready to start on the second stage.

After going a little distance we overtook an Afghan, with his outfit of camels laden with supplies, resting by a bore, he having his breakfast and the camels drinking the refreshing water; they may have a long way to go before they reach the next watering place.

The next night brought us to the Hamilton Bore station, and we were more than thankful for the comfort of a home, for we were very tired after being bumped over miles and miles of stones till we felt that all our joints had worked loose, and we might fall in pieces at any moment.

However, we were so kindly received that we soon forgot our shaking.

The next day brought us to Blood's Creek store, where we spent a very happy evening and comfortable night. Here, too, I recall I was given great encouragement to go forward.

Early the next morning, after a breakfast of ham and eggs and steak, we continued our journey to Charlotte Waters, crossing over the boundary of South Australia and the Northern Territory.

There were no women at Charlotte Waters, but we were received with great kindness by the bachelor officers at the telegraph station. We had lunch and posted letters for the South mail, and sent telegrams.

After resting for a few hours we continued on a few miles, till we reached our camping ground, where we were joined by a party of stockmen returning from Oodnadatta after trucking horses. Here also a fresh batch of horses arrived from Alice Well, sent by the constable in charge, to help us.

So now our combined party had two women, three white men, eight native boys, and thirty-six horses. All travelled as one party till we reached Horseshoe Bend, where the stockmen parted from us to go West to Eldunda.

We crossed the dry bed of the Finke five times, following a winding track. The scenery here is very beautiful, particularly the majestic white gums which grow in the creek bed.

We arrived at Horseshoe Bend very tired and dusty, and I recall with what pleasure we accepted the very hospitable welcome from our host and his wife. How we enjoyed the delicious food, and after an evening of music and friendly talk, how we rested in that comfortable room, with its spotless white linen and curtains.

All must admire the courage of these men and women who build such homes in these remote places.

Although there were a number of drovers and stockmen about the hotel, we did not see or hear one indication of drinking. The whole night was perfectly quiet except for the occasional barking of dogs at the natives' camp, and at dawn the faint sound of a distant fowl-yard.

The new day was to be the most trying for our horses and driver, for we were to pass over unusual country—twenty miles of nothing but sand-hills.

For the whole day long, from morning till night, nothing to be seen but one sand ridge after another, up and down, again up and again down. When down nothing could be seen but the skyline above the next ridge, and when up the eye reached over many miles of barren sand-hills in every direction.

After toiling over ten miles, we rested a while for lunch and a change of horses, in sight of some grand desert oaks.

When we had passed over another five miles with our fresh team, we had an experience which, in a measure, relieved the monotony of sand-hills.

On the North side of a hill there lies a narrow creek bed, the crossing of which, with our load, needed the setting off from the top of the hill at a hand gallop, which our driver did—the native boy, for some reason, being sent on in front.

Gathering up the reins for the descent and sending on his team in good style, we were almost at the bottom of the incline when the horses in the lead stopped dead, and the speed of the pole horses and weight of the buggy sent the pole in amongst the leaders' legs. The leaders jumped out of the traces and went back up the hill, taking the pole horses around with them, they being controlled by nothing but the tangled reins, the driver having been thrown out on to his head at the first bump.

The native boy, seeing what had happened, came racing back on his horse in time to meet our driver righting his team—I, still perched up on the bedding, wondering what I should do in such an emergency.

However, the pole horses behaved well, and all was soon put right, and we were well on our way again, our driver making light of his hurt.

We soon reached the bachelor home of the constable at Alice Well, and were made welcome to the best that he had, and were shown the working of the well by a team of donkeys, and a very fine vegetable garden.

Early the next day we began a long drive to our next open camp, where once again our tent was put up and the fire lighted. Here we tasted for the first time camp-oven bread. It is made in this way: A hole is dug in the ground and filled with hot coals. When the earth is quite hot, the hot oven is placed in, the dough is put in, and the lid replaced. The oven is then covered with coals on top and around its sides, the whole then being made airtight with earth. This mound is carefully watched to see that no faint streak of smoke should appear. Should this happen, however, more earth is at once patted on to the mound where the smoke appears, to prevent the bread burning at that place.

The bread was good, and we spent a very pleasant evening around the camp fire.

The next day's journey brought us to Deep Well by noon. Here we were made welcome by the owner and his wife and their charming children, and we spent some hours of very pleasant fellowship. We then passed on our way, after thanking these kind, hospitable bush people, and made camp a few miles further on. The next two days were very pleasant travelling, and we found those plains all that we had been led to expect. Also we could see the Macdonnell Range in the distance. We had come to our last camp. The next day we would be at the end of our journey.

Although in the heart of the Continent, this was the most pleasant part of the journey; perhaps because of the sight of those majestic ranges, their height and ruggedness was very refreshing after having left the last hills seven hundred miles behind us—Flinders Range.

This is the day on which we are to arrive at Alice Springs: we have been on the road for nine days. We are full of expectation.

The " Gap " in the range through which we pass is certainly beautiful, as are the hills all around when one has passed through on to the North side. About two miles farther on there lies the little settlement of Alice Springs.

This time, however, is not favourable for a first sight of this place, as the country is in the midst of a drought, with all the ugliness and discomfort that a drought can bring—dust, flies, and dying stock.

I had been told much about the beauty of this place, and felt a keen disappointment. Nor was I ever to see those Ranges and country at their best, as the drought lasted till after my departure eleven months later, with only one good rain, which quickly soaked into the parched ground.

What met my eye on passing through the beautiful gap was a dirty sandy flat about two miles

SHEDS FOR THE HALF-CASTE CHILDREN.

North and South, and a little more East and West, surrounded by the main range on the South and West and broken stony hills on the North and East.

On the left one passes a well and troughs for watering stock; a natives' camp with a few stray natives about, and their starving dogs. On the North side is another natives' camp. And in the midst of all lies the little white settlement, made up of seven houses, including two private houses, two stores, a hotel, policeman's houses, Chinese and Afghans' houses; also two corrugated iron sheds for the half-caste children.

Our buggy and accompanying cavalcade at last drew up to the house where I was to board for five months.

During these months I tried to understand the needs of the people, both white and black. I had seen a little of life in the country in Victoria, but this is not Victorian bush, but an entirely new Australia —quite different from anything that I had known. And although I had been on the fringe of it at Oodnadatta for one and a half years, I was yet to experience what it means to be utterly alone, without any means of escape from an isolated position— isolated in every sense.

Men went North and South with camels, but it was eight months after I reached Alice Springs before the next horses and buggy passed over that drought-stricken country.

I had come here for a definite purpose—just to live here for one year as best I could, in order to discover the conditions and needs, from the point of view of a nurse. And at the end of the year to report as to the usefulness of putting a nursing home here similar to the Hostel in Oodnadatta.

Something, obviously, was needed to make things more safe for these brave men and women who had settled in distant parts far out on stations off the overland route. But just how much could be done by a nurse unaided was the question; and could her own nerves stand the strain of the isolation and lack of proper food?

The first local vehicle in Oonadatta, 1915.

ALICE SPRINGS.

CHAPTER V

NATIVES, DUST-STORM, AND BURIAL PLACE

AFTER the first few weeks I began to see why I had been advised not to come by so many people further South. However, I had undertaken to stay for one year, and for one year I would stay if it were humanly possible.

In my many lonely wanderings I visited the local burial place, where I found evidence of the many who had passed by that way and had fallen—the story of their suffering and endurance for ever untold.

Going often to the top of a high hill which overlooks the settlement, I followed with my eye the course of the creek bed, and pictured all those brave men and women who had passed over this creek during the past fifty years, or had followed its course in their, more or less, successful quest for home and treasure.

I waylaid native women and tried to know them better.

Sometimes they were sad, but more often they responded with a gay laugh. They are childlike and cheerful. They are lifted up or cast down according to the measure of their food supply.

I wandered about the hills enjoying the solitude, at times being accompanied by newly-made friends.

My most frequent walk took me to the telegraph station, to a class of white children on Sundays, and to post letters and send wires on other days. The mother of these children was a brave little English

"OVER A STONY RISE BESIDE THE CREEK."

woman, who had come from England and gone forth with her husband into wild and unknown country where no other white woman had previously dared to go, and had taken her three little children with her. This walk takes one along a track skirting the creek bed, and passing over small stony rises all the way. At one part it passes through the midst of the natives' camp at the edge of the creek bed.

They get their water supply from a soakage which they make in the creek bed.

To one not accustomed to the place and people it gave, at first, an eerie feeling to meet on some lonely spot. and hidden from view till one was close upon them, a company of natives, scantily clad and having their hands filled with spears. But in time one grows accustomed to such sights, and when passing give them a friendly nod or good-day.

I had had to deal with a few natives in Oodnadatta, but the close proximity of these camps was something new, and I was somewhat afraid of meeting with them in their more native state.

One day, when close to the natives' camp, I met with a strange and, to me, fearsome looking cow. Now, I never care to meet with a strange cow in any part of the country unless there is also a fence handy—there is no fence in Central Australia.

This cow looked at me with suspicion, turned around and pranced, turned again and again pranced, put down her head and watched me. I stood like a statue and watched the cow, which shook its head and again pranced—this was quite enough; I gathered together my skirt and made one wild, terrified rush right into the midst of the natives' camp, for once forgetting my fear of them.

They had been watching, and had seen what happened, and stood about their humpies with their miserable dogs walking around. waiting to see how I would deal with the situation.

So that when I fled into their midst in that wild way, they waved their arms above their heads and rocked and rolled with laughter.

I was indignant at such untimely mirth, and said: " I have been frightened by that cow." When they could control their mirth sufficiently to be able to speak they gasped out: " That cow been frighten longa you."

Then one dusky girl came to my aid, and said with a most sympathetic air: " You frighten? Me go longa you." She proceeded to accompany me on my way. When I reached the telegraph station, and was parting with my escort, I handed her some pennies.

On the return journey, a couple of hours later, half the female portion of the camp was out waiting to accompany me home again. There were no more pennies, but a few sweets did just as well.

Ever after this I never went out without a supply of sweets. For never after this did I lack an escort whatever direction I might take. And those simple women saw to it that some harmless little calf, or half-starved cow, was somewhere in my path, as an excuse for their offer to accompany me. However, I was grateful for their simple act of friendliness.

After boarding for a little over six months I was able, by the thoughtful and generous act of a gentleman at Arltunga, to take my few belongings and make a home in a small cottage of three rooms, where for part of the time I had the help and companionship of a half-caste native woman named Maudie.

"MY CABIN."

My new home might look, to southern eyes, a very poor little cabin, but I was glad to have it.

As the year advances and no rain has come, the dust storms grow worse. Towards the close of one very hot day we heard a roaring sound and other indications of the approach of a dust storm. So we hurry on with the evening meal and get all crockery and food tightly under cover before the dust is upon us. Then we listen and watch, and, as the time passes, we see to the South, swirling high above the mountain range, one huge wall of brown sand—miles of it—the whole length of the range as far as one could see. On and on it comes, gaining force as it advances, roaring and raging. Dogs go into hiding, horses and camels tremble and become restless. We shut doors and windows, and go into the stifling heat of the house.

It is upon us at last, and in spite of doors and windows—or because of them—the dust pours in. I cover up my head in a pillow case and wait, feeling that the house must be swept away. Hour after hour through the night it rages. I beat with my hands on the partition dividing our room, and beg Maudie not to go to sleep, for I feel that I shall not be able to breathe much longer. But the sound of even breathing tells me that the storm is not keeping Maudie awake.

In time it has spent its fury, and subsides. Then follows flashes of lightning and peals of thunder, which seem to come from every direction. As this, in turn, subsides, a few drops of rain fall, not enough to damp the ground. The remainder of the night

THE BURIAL PLACE. ALICE SPRINGS.

is quiet, and the morning dawns bright and clear, with a warm, pleasant sunshine.

But how the poor cattle did need the rain to make the grass spring up. It was pitiful to see their starved condition.

Fine vegetable gardens are drooping because of the storm. Cabbages, tomatoes, onions, silver beet and grape vines all flat and wilted. At dawn, native boys have begun to carry water in the hope of yet saving them.

The burial place lay half a mile to the west of the settlement, and is marked by two old iron-bark trees, through the leaves of which the wind utters a mournful sighing.

Some of the graves have walls built of stone hewn out of the mountain side. Others have a post and rail fence, with rough crosses formed from a broken bedstead, with no word to indicate who lies there. Others have very fine stones.

One I note bears this inscription: " F.R.G. This is the grave of a man who was a geological and mining surveyor in the Mines Department, who had been sent out as a leader of a prospecting expedition. Starting west from Oodnadatta to the Peterman Ranges, they met with trouble from wild natives, two of the party being badly speared. The leader then made in for Alice Springs, but unfortunately took ill, dying a few days later from heart failure. He had with him a white man as cook."

Then follow stones indicating the resting-places of a man aged sixty-eight and of a woman aged thirty years.

The next is in memory of J.C.K. A beautiful stone and an iron railing almost buried by sand-drift. This was a young stockman, quite a boy, employed by the Pastoral company. At the time of his death he was working at Temple Bar well, which had been lying idle about holiday time. When work

TEMPLE BAR GAP.

began again this young, inexperienced boy was sent down in a bucket. At the bottom he met with foul air, and fell out and died before he could be rescued by his brother, who went down after him.

Lying on the ground in the wooden box which encased it years ago, but which is now crumbling away from it, and placed over no grave, is a roughly hewn stone bearing this inscription: " In memory of J.C. This stone was erected by public subscription in recognition of his sportsmanlike qualities and general good fellowship." The body, I am told, is buried one hundred miles out West.

It took so long to get the stone up from the South that those responsible for raising the subscription had left the district and others had lost interest. After being carried the various stages from the head of the railway by friendly people coming that way, a team had finally drawn in and dumped it down at this burial place, in the hope that other sympathetic people would do the rest.

The object of all this kindly thought was an old man of sixty years, the owner of Granite Downs station, sixty miles west of Alice Springs. He died in his camp, after suffering for a long time. He was an Irishman who had arrived in this country in the early seventies. Being full of kindness and wit, he had many friends.

Arthur, the Mail Boy at Stuart's Creek.

CHAPTER VI

THE BREAKING OF THE DROUGHT

MUCH care is taken by the Government to protect and care for little half-caste children. Two of these little girls were brought into the children's sheds in Alice Springs from a distant tribe, but being strangers, and not understanding the children with whom they were placed, they ran away before daylight one morning.

The police trackers were sent after them, and they were found twelve miles away, and five miles from the nearest water, exhausted.

They had taken off their clothes and buried their little bodies in the sand to protect them from the burning sun and scorching wind.

For all of these unfortunate little children, both boys and girls, a Christmas treat is provided, and the men of the settlement get up sports for them at the New Year season. In 1916 there were thirty-five of these children in the sheds.

Central Australia is a land of beautiful sunsets, and the restfulness of seeing them towards evening seems to compensate for the discomfort of a scorching day of dust and flies. In the evening the air is cool, and beautiful lizards scamper about the rocks on the hills.

"BURIED THEIR BODIES IN THE SAND."

It was about the middle of the month of June. After a day spent in attending to some minor ailments, and the doing of some tooth extractions, I sat in the front of my little cottage in a deck-chair—the gift of a bushman—and watched the sun set. The whole Western sky was lit up with gold of a rich shade. There were sheets of blue-grey clouds bordered with pale gold and flecked with all shades of blue, and a background of neutral green-blue. Far on the outer edge were dark grey clouds, their borders touched with dark pink. As its beauty quickly passed from view, a gloom spread over the whole sky, till the pale moon appeared and was from time to time hidden behind dark and broken clouds.

Sitting on a boulder on the hillside one evening in the month of February, and watching daylight fade, I noticed that the natives already had their fires burning, for although the days were hot, the evenings were sharp. These thin, ill-fed people must have fires to keep themselves warm and to cook their evening meal for themselves and their dogs.

I see both camps quite clearly, the little humpies, the groups of frisking, laughing men, women and children, and the dogs foraging around.

As dusk sets in I see from each home come those who have been employed during the day, bearing with them any scraps of food which otherwise would go into the waste bucket. A few bones, a goat's trotters, inside organs—anything. What the natives do not eat the dogs will have. Flour, tea, sugar, fat, stale bread; however little it is, it goes into the general meal for this dark community.

NEW YEAR SPORTS.

As they wend their way to the camp they call happily to each other and talk at a distance by signs. They are on familiar ground, and understand each other. They also have a subtle way of knowing all that is going on in the white people's world, either for good or ill.

As I sat alone an old woman came out of her course to speak to me. On she came, carrying a jam tin of flour and the head of a goat. Leaping with bare feet from one rock to another, ignoring the pathway, at last she stood before me and said, " Good-day." I replied: " Good-day, Triff, you look happy; sit down." Down she curled on the stone beside me. She obviously had something on her mind, and I kept silent. Presently she put her hand gently on my shoulder and said: " Poor Nussa all alone; that no good. One fella all alone; that no good."

This simple old native touched on part of the problem of a nurse in the Centre—" One fella all alone, no good."

On the evening of 5th March, 1916, we experienced another dust-storm, but this time it was followed by a good rain. When the dust had gone down came the rain, and plenty of it—the first rain for many months. Down it poured hour after hour. It came down the chimney and splashed across the floor from the big, open fire-place.

The morning came bright and fine, with signs and sounds of life everywhere. The long-looked-for day had come for the natives to go out into the bush to catch food, and to fish in the creek for snakes and other live creatures which accompany a flooded creek.

The white population is expectant of grass for the stock, which may mean that we shall get a little mutton or beef, and perhaps a little butter, a luxury which I had not had for many months.

However, there is no meat yet, not even goat, so we have our breakfast of porridge with goats' milk, tea and bread and jam.

As the dinner hour approached I sent Maudie to the store for a tin of meat, and she returned waving a leg of goat in her hand and a look of pure delight on her face. Our neighbour at the store, with his usual kindness, sent us of the best that he had. Poor Maudie, she had begun to believe that she would never see a bit of meat again.

The next day found the creek still running, and as the goats were on the opposite side from us, we could not get any milk to-day. However, two days later saw the creek clear of water again, and an abundance of milk to be had. Also, there was indication of more rain. At four o'clock in the afternoon the rain came down in a torrent.

Our two slab rooms are about twenty feet from the kitchen, with no shelter between.

On came the rain, with lightning and crashes of thunder, and higher and higher rose the lake of water about our cabin. The table for my evening meal was set ready, and Maudie had a fire in the kitchen. But the rain became heavier and the storm more fierce. Taking off my shoes, I dashed through

the water which separated us, in the vain hope of
being able to get on with the cooking of the meal,
for we were very hungry.

Maudie had the supper prepared for cooking, but
what was happening to our fire? The rain coming
down the wide chimney was putting it all out. And
the water had risen over the doorstep and was racing

"DECIDED TO SEE THE CREEK IN FLOOD."

over the earthen floor and swamping our little pile
of firewood. The soot was splashing over everything.

As there seemed no sign of the storm and rain
subsiding, I took off my shoes again and waded
out to find planks to bridge the distance between our
kitchen and dining room. After a lot of wading
about I had managed to construct a fairly reliable

bridge—reliable, provided that Maudie did not put her weight too suddenly upon the weak parts.

A few days later one of the village men remarked: " I suppose you got a bit of wet around your way." Well, at all events, we got our supper, and before dark decided to see the creek in flood—it had over-flowed its banks.

With the aid of a few boxes and planks we were able to bridge the distance to the gate—and to firm ground. From this we dodged around small lakes till we reached the creek.

What joy to see the rushing torrent racing and roaring by, and carrying along with it all that came in its way.

Everybody is happy and hopeful now, for the present the drought is forgotten, but by no means passed. Still the flies are with us. As I sit in my doorway and listen to the stream roaring by and splashing against the trees, I am obliged to get under a fly net.

The ground is thoroughly soaked, and in a few days the green blades of grass will appear above the earth. All the natives who can get away are going into the bush to get native food.

The nights feel quite close in the house though cool in the open, so we carry out our camp beds every night.

I have been warned to keep watch for snakes since the rain. So every night as we prepare to rest I ask Maudie, " Do you think there are any snakes about? " She laughs, then in sympathy becomes serious. "No, no snake; don't you be frighten, Nussa. I not let anytings hurt you; I got big stick—kill 'em."

The grass which so quickly sprang up after the rain is just as quickly dying off again with the heat of the sun. And the surface of the ground, where the grass is dry, is covered with brown caterpillars, which are being scraped up into vessels by the natives. They roast them on coals and eat them. These caterpillars do not appear where the grass is green and soft, but only where it has become dry.

Yesterday we used up our last bone, and to-day hear that there is no goat in the local market. Something must be done, for there is a cool change, and we are ready to eat anything that looks like meat.

A neighbour's hen has visited us and made a nest amongst some shavings which came up wrapped around some bottles of lotion, and we have one egg which we can share for supper; but what about dinner first?

Even while we consider, the native boy of a neighbour came up with a basket of fresh green beans, also a little pat of butter, the first that we have seen for months, with this simple message: "Jim been send 'em." Exactly like the thoughtful thing Jim would do, we thought.

Now we are right, hot salmon and beans.

But we must, in this climate, have some of the latest supply of salmon that came by the last camel team.

Away went Maudie for the fish while I prepared the beans. She was a long time gone, and I went out to watch for her. Presently she appeared with not only the fish, but carrying something on a dish. What could it be? The huge leg of a wild turkey, steaming hot and nicely cooked, sent by our good friend at the store, and with the North countryman's simple message: " George been send 'em," said Maudie.

CHAPTER VII

RETURNING SOUTH

HOW we live for the coming of the mail-man from the South, and how, since early morning, all eyes have been turned to the South where the mail-man must pass through the gap in the range. "What is this?" some watcher calls, and we shade our eyes and peer towards the gap once more. Yes, at last we see five dark specks moving through the gap. We strain our eyes and look again to be sure that we are not deceived. No, we are not, for soon we recognise the tired stride of the laden camels swinging along with their creaking burdens over that last mile to the settlement.

When they reach the general store the mail-man and his native boy throw off the heavy goods and their own personal belongings, and give any messages picked up between this and the head of the railway. They then hasten on with His Majesty's mail to the post office two miles further on. There they wait for the mail to be sorted and stamped and bring it back to the store.

At the store several hands help in sorting out the papers and parcels, and our trusty storekeeper takes charge of the letter bag. Not till all the papers and parcels are distributed does he open the letter bag.

ALICE SPRINGS HOTEL.

The moment for which we have lived for the last two weeks has arrived. The few white people stand along the counter in a row, while our letters are dealt out like a pack of cards. We grasp at each one as it comes flying over the counter towards us, till all are finished.

I have my letters, and so hurry off home to be quietly with them for a few hours, passing through a row of natives, who lean up against the shop verandah posts getting all the news of the journey from the mail-man's native boy.

The week is then spent in talking over news from the South and preparing our next mail to send away. When it has gone South we just wait again, till once more we strain our eyes to see those specks appearing through the gap.

Two hundred and fifty miles South the drought has quite broken, and it is now possible for horses to pass over to get to Oodnadatta. My good friend, Mrs. R. and her husband, are preparing to go to Adelaide, and I am preparing to go with them. It does not take us long, for we must take as little as possible. The horses are to be considered in every way. It is easy to part with some things, but I look long at my precious books—must I part with them? Yes, they are heavy. Well, plenty of people will value them, and so I pass them on to others.

Eleven months since I came up on that track, and now I am about to return.

The day for departure has arrived, and all is ready. Three of us in the seat and luggage piled high up behind.

Waving good-bye to those men who had proved such friends to me, our lively horses were soon speeding with us towards the gap in the range, through which we must pass to go South.

During that first day I took mental note that Mr. R. was being cramped for room, and hindered

"GAP IN THE RANGE THROUGH WHICH WE PASS."

in his management of the horses, so made up my mind to think out some way of getting myself placed in some other part of the buggy, and so leave him more room.

After our first camp supper an idea came to me, and I asked in a casual way: " What about my riding one of the horses to-morrow? " " Can you ride? "

asked my friends. "It is fifteen years since I tried, but I suppose I can."

It being settled that I should ride, the next thing was to choose a horse from the outfit. "Winkie" was my choice, and Winkie I was promised the next day.

Now Winkie was a splendid mount, but I must remember that he had been trained as a stockman's horse, and I must not waste too much time in mounting, but be prepared for him to go off at the slightest touch of the stirrup.

The next morning I began by ignoring the offered help of the native boy and put on the saddle myself, just to show everybody that they need have no anxiety about me. My friends were busy getting their buggy team ready, and that being completed, Mr. R. turned his attention to helping me into the saddle. "She is up," I heard him exclaim. Good old Winkie had entered into the proper spirit of the occasion, and stood perfectly still while I mounted from a fallen tree. However, there were a few final touches needed. The saddle was a man's, and the stirrups had to be shortened. I was then given a switch, which I was duly warned not to allow Winkie to know about.

Now all was ready, and away swept the buggy in the lead, I following next, and behind came the native boy with the pack horses and remainder of the outfit. Away we cantered. The weather was perfect. We had our backs to the North and were facing the South, and all seemed well.

ON THE JOURNEY SOUTH.

And all was well for the first few miles, till we overtook a herd of cattle being rounded up by drovers. Winkie thought this little bit of cattle chasing was too good to be missed, so he just tossed his head and carried me wherever he liked. I grasped the reins in one hand and the saddle in the other, but forgot to keep the shadow of the switch out of Winkie's line of vision. Over the soft ground we raced, till the drovers, taking in the situation, quietened down their own horses.

Of course, they had no idea that a woman was behind them riding, or they would have prepared for it and taken their herd a little off the track.

It was a relief to get to the end of the first twenty miles, so that we might rest and camp for the night. The third day we reached Deep Well, eighty miles on the way we had come, and so on over the country I had travelled through on the journey North.

After another camp we were well on the way to Marysville station. At this home we spent half an hour talking with these kind, hospitable people, who urged us to come in and rest and take tea. But tired as we were, the day was passing, and we must press on to where there is feed and water for the horses before nightfall. We camped that night, and the end of the next day found us once again in the midst of the twenty miles of sand-hills. The weather was very cold, but we were prepared for cold weather, Mr. and Mrs. R. in their tent, and I on the floor of the buggy, with a sheet of water-proof material thrown over to keep off the heavy dew.

The next evening at Horseshoe Bend we had a little rain, but the sky cleared before we set off on the twenty-one miles' ride, which took us just five hours.

It was becoming more urgent that we should press on, as rain might come at any time and flood the creeks, and so prevent our crossing. Towards nightfall we drew up at Old Crown Point station, a very pretty spot close to the crown point of the mount.

We were startled in the night by hearing a few drops of heavy rain, and strange sounds as, going his weary way, the North mail-man passed us with his five camels.

The slight rain had passed off in the morning, and after a hasty breakfast we passed on by the old deserted homestead, waving as we passed to a company of native women carrying buckets of water on their heads from a well.

After camping at the Goyder crossing, we set out at sunrise, and had the delightful experience of cantering over beautiful green fields all the way to the new Crown Point homestead. No further need for anxiety over grass for the horses now, for good rain had fallen, and there was abundance of green. The weather also was perfect, warm sunshine and keen fresh air.

After resting for two days at the homestead we set off again on another day's journey of thirty miles, passing by Charlotte Waters telegraph station. Here we met again our old friends of the North journey, and although we could not spare time to go in, we were glad to accept the kindly offer of tea, while I remained in the saddle and my friends in their buggy. Passing on over stony ground, we reached a nice fertile spot beside a creek, which was a very pleasant camp, and to the joy of our native boy there were plenty of lizards.

Passing on to the Blood's Creek store for dinner, we were warned that the creek we wished to cross was full of water.

However, we pressed on over the last seven miles which would bring us to Blood's Creek station.

Twenty-seven miles my horse had carried me that day, and at evening we found ourselves faced with a swollen creek from the recent rain.

First the buggy passed over the stream, the horses plunging through with water up to their backs. I made haste to follow, tucking up my feet on the saddle. I followed instructions, allowing Winkie to choose his own way and get over without any directions from me. I was glad when he plunged up the bank on the other side of the stream.

Here, however, I was confronted with another difficulty—wild pigs. Winkie dreads wild pigs. However, I managed to prevent his seeing them and all passed off well.

Arrived at the homestead, we were given a warm welcome. This is a perfectly delightful country home, with many comforts inside and outside. Flower garden, vegetable garden, and always an abundance of water.

"FIRST THE BUGGY PASSED OVER THE STREAM

After staying here for two days our further journey took us through beautiful country—a most pleasant journey. Next night we camped six miles north of Hamilton Bore station. Passing by the homestead next day, we got a supply of meat and fresh bread.

Our horses had now taken us three hundred miles, and we must get them over this stony country to where there is grass and water.

On Friday night, as we were in camp, it was a pleasure to see the faithful animals eating up the delicious fresh grass.

Saturday found us passing slowly over country which had miles and miles of nothing but one stony ridge after another, till we came within a few miles of Oodnadatta, where we came upon a good road.

Cantering easily along on the faithful animal which had brought me over so many miles, and which was, no doubt, as tired as I was, the faithful Winkie stumbled and fell.

As the buggy, with two fresh horses in, had passed over a rise, my plight was not known till Mr. R., looking back, saw my riderless steed with dangling reins following the buggy. Jumping from the buggy and catching the horse, he led him back to look for me, and was relieved to find me running after my mount and quite unhurt.

My friends wanted me to come into the buggy, but I had no mind to make my entry into Oodnadatta other than seated upon Winkie.

There is nothing more to tell of this journey, except our meeting just outside the village the camel mail carrying mails which had arrived at the rail head on the previous night from the South: drovers with cattle to be trucked on Monday, and other

THE CAMEL MAIL.

drovers with sheep and goats, strings of camels, teams of donkeys with white men, native men and Afghans.

A turn in the road brought us in sight of Oodnadatta and in direct touch with—home.

Two policemen at Oonadatta, 1917.

OODNADATTA JACKY.
South Australian Native.

Chas. P. Scott. Photo.
21a Waymouth St.
Adelaide.

Ingram Content Group Australia Pty Ltd
Printed in Australia
AUHW010927270623
380040AU00001B/1

9 781923 024106